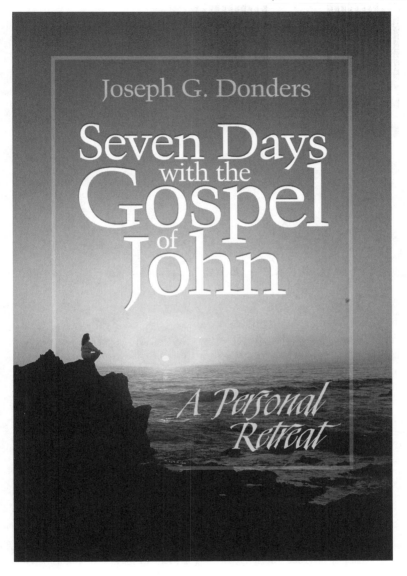

Joseph G. Donders

Seven Days
with the
Gospel
of
John

A Personal Retreat

TWENTY-THIRD PUBLICATIONS

185 WILLOW STREET • PO BOX 180 • MYSTIC, CT 06355
TEL: 1-800-321-0411 • FAX: 1-800-572-0788
E-MAIL: ttpubs@aol.com • www.twentythirdpublications.com

Twenty-Third Publications
A Division of Bayard
185 Willow Street
P.O. Box 180
Mystic, CT 06355
(860) 536-2611
(800) 321-0411
www.twentythirdpublications.com

ISBN:1-58595-254-0
Library of Congress Catalog Card Number: 2002111934
Printed in the U.S.A.

CONTENTS

SUGGESTIONS FOR MAKING A RETREAT

Prepare a quiet place where you can make your retreat. Set up a few symbols that might help create a prayerful atmosphere, such as a statue, a cross, an icon, or a candle. Sit in a comfortable chair. Have a notebook ready to write down your thoughts, feelings, and ideas.

Set a time limit for your reflection; a half-hour to an hour per meditation might do. Use the morning meditation before you begin your day, and the evening meditation either at the end of your work day or before going to bed.

Avoid distractions; try to relax and empty your mind of all worries and concerns. Know that you are in God's presence, that God is present in you, your family, your community, and the world.

Read the Scripture passage cited at the beginning of each meditation. Allow the words to fill your mind. Pause at the words or phrases that speak to you in a particular way, that touch your mind or your heart. Reflect on how the Scripture texts relate to you, your work, your relationships, and your life. The suggestions in the *For Reflection* section will help spark some ideas.

Try to listen to what the Spirit is saying to you. Remember that the most important part of prayer is to be attentive to God's word. Be open to that word, even when it challenges you to live as you have never lived before.

Pray for all those who are making a retreat at the same time as you, and who might even be using this same book. Ask that all of you may be blessed with the knowledge that the Spirit of God is always present, always calling us forward.

Begin a journal that you will use throughout the retreat. Record in it your thoughts and prayers, as well as the moments when you are most aware of God's presence in your life.

INTRODUCTION

John's gospel is an excellent companion for prayer and reflection. It is a treasure chest full of insights and surprises, and therefore, a wonderful retreat guide.

Through the pages of this little book, I invite you to reflect on John's gospel and use it to make a mini-retreat, a prayerful time away in the midst of your daily tasks and responsibilities. This may mean getting up earlier than usual for a morning meditation, and putting aside tasks earlier than usual for an evening meditation.

During this seven-day period we will focus together on the spiritual advice found in the gospel of John. We will follow the developments—the ups and downs—in the discoveries made by the people who surrounded Jesus.

Every book has its own dynamics. Few people would take a book, read one chapter or a few paragraphs from it, then feel they had the whole story. Yet when reading sacred Scripture—including the gospels—we usually read just small fragments: a snippet here and a snippet there. It is not often, for example, that we read a whole gospel from beginning to end. The result is that the inherent meaning and purpose of each book of the Bible can be overlooked.

This is certainly true of the four gospels. Each gospel has its own approach and its own message. Each introduces Jesus in its own way, and is written in response to different needs and different times. Each of the four evangelists tells their story with the desire to help us relate the story to our own lives.

John's gospel reads like a detective story. It is full of questions: "What are you looking for?"; "What have I done for you?"; "Do you love me?"; "Do you now believe?" From the first chapter to the very last, the numerous characters in this gospel slowly discover who Jesus really is. (And the last one to solve that mystery is Thomas, the most famous doubter in Scripture.)

The author of the gospel of John remains a bit of a mystery. Is he Jesus' disciple John, or is he the beloved disciple who is mentioned again and again? These questions are difficult to answer—but they are not the most important, either. Whoever the author was, experts agree that John's gospel was the last one to be written. It differs from the other three, the so-called synoptic gospels. The synoptic gospels pay special attention to Jesus' works and words; you might call them "action" gospels. They easily lend themselves to dramatization, e.g., being made into a movie.

John's gospel takes another approach. In John's work we listen to long discourses in which Jesus reveals what is going on in his heart and mind. Books that describe the inner spiritual development of a person's thoughts and feelings cannot easily be translated into images. They reach out to another level of understanding and insight. Perhaps this is why John's gospel has been considered the favorite among those who meditate on the gospels.

Seven Days with the Gospel of John offers suggestions for a morning and evening meditation. The length of that prayerful reflection can differ from person to person and from community to community, but the ideal would be to spend from half an hour to an hour on each session. You can meditate in the quiet of your room, in a church, or even outside—anywhere you feel prayerfully at home with yourself and God's Spirit. There are also suggested questions for your reflection, to help you consider how John's gospel applies to your everyday life, as well as a morning and evening prayer you can use to end your meditation. Finally, there is a faith response for each of the seven days.

You can make this retreat alone, with a friend, or with several other people. It can also be adapted to seven weeks, or whatever time period suits your needs.

As we make our retreat, we will reflect on some of the main points in the gospel of John. In doing so, we pray that the words of Jesus may affect our lives today as they did the lives of those he touched long ago.

May we come to a new understanding not only of the life of Jesus, but of our own lives, too.

"What are you looking for?"

Read John 1:19–51

The story begins with John the Baptist, the unkempt prophet whom thousands of people from all over are coming to hear. They come because of the hope they have fostered in their hearts, the hope that one day the world—and they themselves—would be changed.

When asked by the priests and Levites whether he was the one to bring about God's reign, John replies that he is not the messiah. He tells them that he can only baptize with water, but that there is one coming after him, one for whom "I am not worthy to untie the thong of his sandal."

The next day, Jesus joins the people gathered around John. He points Jesus out to the crowd saying: "Here is the Lamb of God who takes away the sin of the world! This is he of whom I said, 'After me comes a man who ranks ahead of me because he was before me.'…this is the Son of God."

On the third day (in John's gospel, the third day always indicates the day of fulfillment), Jesus returns for a third time. John repeats what he said the day before: "Look, here is the Lamb of God!" Hearing him say this, two of John's disciples decide to follow Jesus. One of them is Andrew; the other remains unnamed.

Could this unnamed disciple be the one who will be called "the beloved disciple"? Is it John, the author of this gospel? Or is this anonymity an invitation to see ourselves in the place of the unnamed disciple?

Jesus senses that the two are following him, so he turns around and asks, "What are you looking for?" It is one of those questions we hear so often in our lives. We enter a store and look around, and a salesperson asks the same question: "What are you looking for?" The question implies an invitation: "Can I help you?"

Might Jesus be asking you this same question? As you begin this retreat, ask yourself: what am I looking for? Who am I looking for? Do I have the same kind of eagerness to follow Jesus as Andrew and the unnamed disciple?

The two disciples reply to Jesus' question with one of their own: "Rabbi" (which translated means Teacher), "where are you staying?" Jesus said, "Come and see." And this is what they did. So imprinted on their minds was this event that they remembered the exact time of their meeting, four o'clock in the afternoon. They went with Jesus and stayed with him the rest of the day.

It was while staying at Jesus' home that the disciples made up their minds about him. This is interesting to note. People show their true colors when they are at home. Those who are friendly in their relationships with others at work or within the community may be just the opposite at home. So for the disciples, seeing Jesus at home was the true test. They began to believe in him.

Andrew was so impressed with Jesus that he found his brother Simon, and told him, "We have found the Messiah...." He no longer called Jesus "Rabbi." Andrew brought Simon to Jesus, who looked at him and said: "You are Simon, son of John. You are to be called Cephas." This name translates as "Peter"; it also means "rock."

It must have warmed Simon's heart to be called "rock." Here was someone who understood him from their first meeting—just as Jesus had understood Andrew and his companion when he asked them: "What are you looking for?" Jesus knew that they were searching for meaning and fulfillment in their lives.

Jesus must have noticed the same eagerness and hope in Philip, the next disciple whom he finds. Jesus simply says, "Follow me." And Philip did, though surely he did not understand what lay ahead.

When Philip then finds Nathanael, he tells him, "We have found him...." But this is not quite true; it is Jesus who has found them. Neither did Philip understand exactly who he was following. He tells Nathanael that he had found the one about whom Moses and the prophets had been writing, adding that he is "Jesus son of Joseph from Nazareth."

When Nathanael answered: "Can anything good come from Nazareth?" Philip replies with the words Jesus speaks at the beginning of this account: "Come and see."

When they meet, Jesus boosts Nathanael's ego, so to speak, by saying, "Here is truly an Israelite in whom there is no deceit!" When Nathanael asks him, "Where did you get to know me?" Jesus explains, "I saw you under the fig tree before Philip called you." It is anybody's guess what Nathanael had been doing under that fig tree, but for Nathanael himself Jesus' remark was sufficient to cause him to exclaim: "Rabbi, you are the Son of God. You are the King of Israel!"

Jesus warns Nathanael, however, that he does not yet see the full picture: "Do you believe because I told you that I saw you under the fig tree? You will see greater things than these....you will see heaven opened and the angels of God ascending and descending upon the Son of Man." Indeed, Jesus was true to his word. We will meet Nathanael again in John's last chapter, at the last breakfast Jesus has with his disciples.

How wonderful to see the way Jesus builds these relationships in John's first chapter. It shows how he relates to those he meets, affirming them and lifting them up to the fullness of their calling. In these interactions we see how Jesus relates to us as well.

What a friend we have in Jesus!

FOR REFLECTION

- Why are you making this retreat? What do you hope to accomplish during this time?

- At this point in your life, how would you respond to Jesus' question: "What are you looking for?"

- What word or phrase would you use to express your relationship with Jesus? What kind of relationship do you hope for?

MORNING PRAYER

Jesus, you invite me to "Come and see." As I reflect on your life and on your words during this retreat, help me to know that all I seek rests in you alone.

FAITH RESPONSE FOR TODAY

Render an extra act of kindness to someone at work or at home who recently may have offended you in some way.

"Do whatever he tells you."

Read John 2:1–12; 4:1–43

The first passage for this evening begins, "On the third day there was a wedding in Cana of Galilee." Recall that the third day is used by John to indicate the time of fulfillment.

This passage introduces us to the mother of Jesus, the first woman mentioned in John's gospel. Mary is at the wedding with Jesus and his first followers. The wine gave out and there was only water left, so Mary went to Jesus and said, "They have no wine." That is all she said.

What did she mean? Was she hinting at something more than just a lack of wine on that occasion? Was she also referring to the way the prophets described the messianic times, the hour portrayed by Isaiah as a wedding feast, marking the union between God and God's people? Isaiah had written: "As the bridegroom rejoices over the bride, so will your God rejoice in you" (62:5). Had he also not foretold that those days would be overflowing with wine?

Did Mary feel that the hour had come for her Son to begin the fulfillment of his messianic mission? When she visited her cousin Elizabeth, she had expressed her belief in Jesus as messiah with the glorious words of her magnificat (Lk 1:46–55). The world would be changed by the one she had conceived in her womb. Justice would reign, and the old promises would be fulfilled. Was this to happen now, at this wedding? Was it now that the messianic wine, the wine of the promise, was going to flow?

When Mary went to Jesus and said, "They have no wine," he replied, "My hour has not yet come." This was a rebuttal and yet a promise: his hour would indeed come!

Mary entrusts herself totally to Jesus. When she goes to the servants, she invites them—and us: "Do whatever he tells you." These are the last words Mary speaks in John's gospel. They are an invitation that still reaches us today.

The water was brought out from the kitchen, and Jesus changed it into wine. The disciples witnessed this and did as Mary had done: they believed in him.

Later in John's gospel, Jesus meets a second woman. We do not know her name. Could this be a suggestion that we identify with her? We do know the time and the place: it is midday in Sichar in Samaria, not far from the ruins of the old, plundered Samaritan temple.

Jesus was tired and thirsty. He stopped at an ancient well, one that dated back to the time of Jacob. He was alone; his disciples had gone to look for something to eat. A woman came along; she too was alone. This was strange because the well would have been the only place to get water, and consequently, there were usually people around. Was the woman alone by choice, because of her personal situation?

Jesus asks the woman for some water. In reply, the woman boldly asks how he, a Jew, could request something like that from a Samaritan, since Jews do not share things in common with Samaritans. Jesus then tells her that he can give her "living water." Calling him "Sir," the woman asks how he can do this, since he has no bucket. But Jesus is speaking about the water he can give as a gift of God. He adds that, for those who drink it, this water will become "a spring of water gushing up to eternal life."

Jesus then asks the woman to call her husband. She answers: "I have no husband." Jesus replies that she is right about that, because she has had five husbands and is now living with someone she did not marry. At this point the woman diplomatically changes the subject. She asks a religious question about worship, calling Jesus not only "Sir" but also "prophet": "Sir, I can see you are a prophet. Our ancestors worshiped on this mountain, but you say that the place where people must worship is in Jerusalem."

Jesus answers her question by telling her that the time has come for all to worship the Father in spirit and truth. She responds by telling him that she knows the Messiah is coming and "will proclaim all things to us." It is then that Jesus says something he has not said before: he tells the woman that he is the Messiah. He says: "I am he, the one who is speaking to you."

At that point in the story the disciples join Jesus at the well. When they see him talking to the woman—a Samaritan woman at that!—they are embarrassed and indignant. The woman must have felt their reaction because she left in such a hurry that she forgot to take her water jar with her.

Back home in Sichar, the woman repeats the phrase we have read twice before in our meditations. She says to the people of the city, "Come and see...." "Come and see a man who told me everything I have ever done! He cannot be the Messiah, can he?" Because of the woman's testimony, a crowd from Sichar goes "on their way to him."

Meanwhile, Jesus' disciples urge him to eat, but he tells them, "My food is to do the will of him who sent me and to complete his work." That work is to gather together the people of all nations.

When the Samaritans reach Jesus, they ask Jesus to stay and he does, for two days. They come to believe in him. They tell the woman, "It is no longer because of what you said that we believe, for we have heard for ourselves, and we know that this is truly the Savior of the world!"

This should be our statement as well. We must hear for ourselves and believe, not believe because of what others tell us.

The unnamed Samaritan woman—legend has given her the name Saint Photine—could be considered the one who organized the first community of believers. Through her testimony, others came to see and to believe.

Mary and the Samaritan woman at the well: two faithful disciples who came to believe, and who showed the way to the truth that is Jesus.

FOR REFLECTION

• Mary said at the wedding feast at Cana, "Do whatever he tells you." What do these words mean for you personally? When might Jesus be speaking to you in your daily routine?

• When you talk with others about your relationship with Jesus, do you invite them to, "Come and see" as the Samaritan woman did? Do your actions reflect your faith (e.g., by your kindness, honesty, or acts of social justice)?

- What does it mean to your life today to say that Jesus is the Messiah, the anointed one?

"Do you want to be made well?"

Read John 4:46–53; 5:1–18; 9:1–41

Only three cures are recorded in John's gospel. In chapter four a royal official asks Jesus for help because his son is sick; in chapter five Jesus approaches a lame man who has lain at the pool of Bethesda for thirty-eight years, waiting for a cure; and in chapter nine Jesus encounters a man who has been blind since birth. In all three cases Jesus works a miracle. He cures each of the three: the sick son, the paralyzed man, and the blind beggar. But only two of these people are healed.

The word "healing" is related to the word "whole," while the word "cure" comes from a word that means "to take care of." You can be cured without being healed—and you can be healed without being cured!

Have a look at the three stories to see the difference. The first miracle is the simplest one. A father comes to Jesus because his son—later in the text he is called a little boy—is dying. He asks Jesus to cure his son, to bless him, touch him, do something, but please, heal him. Jesus tells him: "Unless you see signs and wonders you do not believe." The man says: "Sir, come down before my little boy dies." Jesus tells him, "Go, your son will live."

The official believes Jesus and goes home. Before he is even there, his servants come running up to meet him and tell him that his son is alive! The official then asks when the fever had left the boy. It's a superfluous question: he must have known the answer. The child was cured at the moment Jesus had told the official to go home.

Yet more than that cure took place. Because of what Jesus had done, the whole family believed; they were healed.

Many people suffer from illness, allergies, or infections; most are hoping for a cure. But would a cure alone really heal them? Doctors and physicians might be able to cure you; only God heals. Do you want to risk being healed?

"Do you want to be made well?" This is the question Jesus asks the paralyzed man at the pool of Bethesda. The man does not answer "Yes." Instead he avoids the question by saying, "Sir, I have no one to put me into the pool when the water is stirred up; and while I am making my way, someone else steps down ahead of me." Here he refers to an old story about the pool, that now and then an angel of the Lord would come to stir the water and the first one in the pool would be healed.

The man had been lying near the pool for thirty-eight years. He must have become accustomed to his situation. Did he really want to be healed, start anew in life with all the responsibilities this would bring?

Do you know people who are sick and who do not want to be rid of their malady? Oh, they might say that they would like to be cured. Yet this might mean such a change in their lives that they choose not to face it.

What about you? Do you want to be healed, to be whole, to be (w)holy? Are you like the young Augustine, who prayed to be healed of his immorality, then added, "but not yet"?

When the crippled man does not answer in a straightforward manner, Jesus issues a command: "Stand up, take your mat and walk!" And that is what the man does. But we can wonder: does he do so reluctantly? The man walks away from Jesus; he does not follow him. In fact, he would even betray Jesus.

The man had been healed on the Sabbath. As he walked away from the pool, some passersby who were strict observers of the law asked what he was doing: "It is the sabbath; it is not lawful for you to carry your mat." The man answered, "The man who made me well said to me, 'Take up your mat and walk.'" When they asked who that man was, he told them that he did not know him.

Later, the man again met Jesus, this time in the temple. Jesus told him, "See, you have been made well! Do not sin any more, so that nothing worse happens to you." (This does not mean that what might happen to him would be a punishment for his behavior, but a consequence, just as smokers have to suffer the consequences of smoking.)

The cured man then goes off and tells the people that it was Jesus who had cured him, though he must have understood that saying this would cause difficulty for Jesus.

The man had been cured, but he was not healed. He refused to believe. He never called Jesus anything but "that man." He did not go any further.

In the third story of a cure, however, the blind man does go further. When Jesus passes him on the road, his disciples take the occasion to ask Jesus whether the man's parents or he himself had committed a sin that caused him to be born blind. This reflected a common belief of the time, that one's afflictions were the result of the sins of one's parents or oneself.

Jesus tells the disciples that there is no causal connection between sin and suffering. Then, turning to the blind man he spits on the ground, makes some mud with his saliva, and smears it over the man's eyes. He then tells the man to wash his eyes in the pool of Siloam.

Why did Jesus cure the man this way? Why didn't he just command the man to see, as he had commanded the paralyzed man to walk? We do not know the answer. Perhaps it was because the blind man and the people around him expected that this was how a cure should work. Perhaps Jesus was adapting himself to their expectations, traditions, and culture.

When the blind man's neighbors asked him who had cured him, he answered, "the man called Jesus." But when the Pharisees later asked him the same question on two different occasions, he answered that Jesus was "a prophet" and "a man from God." Finally, the man meets Jesus again, and Jesus asks him whether he believes in him, the Son of Man. The man answers, "Lord, I believe!"

This man was not only cured, he was healed!

FOR REFLECTION

- Think about what it means to be a true follower of Christ. What hinders you, paralyzes you, or blinds you in your efforts to follow him more clearly?

- Of what do you want to be cured in your life right now? In what ways do you need to be healed?

- Jesus is asking you, "Do you want to be made well?" How might your life change if you say "yes"?

MORNING PRAYER

Dear Jesus, let me know where I need healing in my life. Give me the courage to ask for your healing and transforming power.

FAITH RESPONSE FOR TODAY

Take time today to call, write, or visit someone you know who is sick or suffering in some way.

"Where are we to buy bread?"

Read John 6:1–40

John's gospel, like the other three, is not very long. You can read any one of the gospels easily during one morning or evening. But because they are so short, every word and every expression is important.

There is another reason why we must pay careful attention to each word or phrase used in the gospels. They contain reminiscences and memories of those who first read and heard these stories.

Let's look at the beginning of the story in chapter six. "After this Jesus went to the other side of the Sea of Galilee, also called the Sea of Tiberias." The "Sea of Tiberias" is, in fact, a lake in Palestine. But when John writes that Jesus is crossing a sea, it reminds those first readers that their ancestors walked out of Egypt and into freedom through the Red Sea. This reference is a sign that at this point in the gospel a new period is about to begin. The crossing of the Sea of Tiberias is a momentous event.

The people on the other side of the lake are hungry. (There are still hungry people in our midst today. At least a third of the people in the world go hungry each day. Every twenty-four hours, thousands of children die of starvation.)

In the midst of those hungry people, Jesus asks Philip, "Where are we to buy bread for these people to eat?" Philip answers that "six months' wages would not buy enough bread for each of them to get a little." Then Andrew—a person John often associates with Philip—says, "There is a boy here who has five barley loaves and two fish. But what are they among so many people?"

It is amazing to think that only one boy would have had some food with him! Was he the only generous soul in that enormous crowd, the only one who was willing to share the food he had brought?

Jesus then exercises some crowd control and asks the people to sit down. Once they are seated, he begins to share the boy's bread and fish among the five thousand. It is interesting to note that in John's gospel, he distributes the food himself; he does not ask his disciples to do it.

When everyone is satisfied, the remaining food is gathered together. The result is an enormous doggy bag, twelve baskets full!

That afternoon Jesus satisfied the very real hunger of the people. Thus they understood that in Jesus a prophet had come into the world. He offered them a quick solution to a problem that is still haunting humanity: the poverty and hunger that are root causes of the terror in our day and age. No wonder the people of Jesus' time wanted to make him their king! (In all the excitement, however, the generosity of the boy who had given Jesus his bread and fish was totally forgotten.)

As the story continues, we see that the disciples are in a hurry to get to the other side of the lake. They take their boat back across, leaving Jesus behind. But the disciples have a rough trip ahead of them. Darkness falls and they encounter strong headwinds. Rowing with all their might they suddenly see a man walking over the water—a preview of the risen Lord!

Not recognizing Jesus immediately, they are terrified at the sight. But Jesus speaks to them with words that are used throughout the gospels: "It is I! Do not be afraid!" The boat arrives safely on the other shore.

The next day the crowd is back again, looking for more. They want to receive bread from heaven, just as their ancestors received manna in the desert. Jesus answers that this type of miracle is not going to be repeated. He tells the people that *he* is the bread from heaven:

I am the bread of life. Your ancestors ate the manna in the wilderness and they died. This is the bread that comes down from heaven, so that one may eat of it and not die. I am the living bread that came down from heaven. Whoever eats of this bread will live forever; and the bread that I will give for the life of the world is my flesh....Those who eat my flesh and drink my blood abide in me, and I in them.

The people around him protest. "Is not this Jesus, the son of Joseph, whose father and mother we know? How can he now say, 'I have come down from heaven'?" When he insists, they add, "This teaching is difficult; who can accept it?" and they start to leave. They do not understand what he is telling them. They have no idea about the way the risen Lord will remain with them. Even his disciples do not understand.

Jesus is aware that his disciples do not understand and that they have the same complaint as those who were leaving him. So he asks the twelve: "Do you also wish to go away?" Peter answers him, "Lord, to whom can we go? You have the words of eternal life. We have come to believe and know that you are the Holy One of God."

We are in a different situation from the people Jesus spoke to in those days. They had not yet been with him at the last supper. We know more about the events that were to come than did the twelve at that moment. We know that Jesus has remained with us in the Eucharist.

To partake of this Eucharist means that we become part of the body of Christ. This is made clear in a quote from Augustine, cited in the *Catechism of the Catholic Church* (#1396):

> If you are the body and members of Christ, then it is your sacra-
> ment that is placed on the table of the Lord; it is your sacrament
> that you receive. To that which you are you respond "Amen" ("yes,
> it is true!") and by responding to it you assent to it. For you hear
> the word "the Body of Christ" and respond "Amen." Be then a
> member of the Body of Christ that your *Amen* may be true.

FOR REFLECTION

- Imagine that you were present when Jesus distributed the bread and the fish, and when he spoke of himself as the bread of life. What might your reaction have been?

- We believe that Jesus Christ is present to us today in the Eucharist. How might you be called to share this presence with others?

- What do you think Augustine means when he says, "it is your sacrament that you receive. To that which you are you respond 'Amen' ('yes, it is true!') and by responding to it you assent to it"?

EVENING PRAYER

Dear Jesus, let me be aware of my physical and spiritual relationship with you. Let me share your life with others as you shared our life during your time here on earth.

"Do you also want to go away?"

Read John 6:16–71

Yesterday we ended our reflection and prayer by reminding ourselves that we are members of the body of Christ. We belong together, but it is even more than that. Together we form one organism. Sometimes we call this togetherness the mystical body of Christ.

Jesus uses a different metaphor to express this reality when he says in John's gospel, "I am the vine, you are the branches. Those who abide in me and I in them bear much fruit, because apart from me you can do nothing" (15:5). In essence, this is what Jesus said about the effect of eating his flesh and drinking his blood: "Those who eat my flesh and drink my blood abide in me, and I in them" (6:56).

Together we form the one body of Jesus Christ. As Paul teaches the Corinthians throughout his letters to them, we should discern that body in our daily life. Sometimes our awareness that we are part of the mystical body gets lost in our comings and goings. But at other times, the reality of Christ's body suddenly shines through the humdrum of life.

I experienced this during the Second World War. I was a boy back then, living in the Netherlands, which was occupied by foreign troops. We considered the soldiers who occupied the country as enemies. We would never accept anything from them nor would we ever eat with them. When we saw others doing that, we considered them traitors who should be punished when the war was over.

We lived under a curfew, and no one was allowed to move through the streets from sunset to sunrise. But in 1943, the foreign military commander, who must have been a Catholic, lifted the curfew for Christmas night.

That night we all went to midnight Mass. I was an altar server and assisted at the Mass. Part of my task was to hold the paten, a small gilded dish, under the hands of the priest while he was distributing communion to the people.

At the beginning of Mass, we heard quite a commotion in the back of the church. About twenty soldiers were stomping around, making a racket with their hobnailed boots. As they entered the church, they put their guns in a back corner with a guard posted in front of them.

At communion time, I accompanied the priest in distributing communion until it appeared all the parishioners had received the Eucharist. I brought the paten back up to the altar, then came back and knelt at the communion rail so that I could receive the host. Suddenly, a small group of soldiers came forward from the back of the church. One knelt down on my right side and two knelt at my left. I could smell the leather of their belts.

Our parish priest, who, at the risk of his life, had helped hide a Jewish family from the occupying forces and who definitely did not like the foreign army, gave communion first to the soldier next to me, then to me, and then to the other two.

At that moment, young as I was, receiving communion with those hostile soldiers, I realized that the body of Christ transcends the human condition. Despite our divisions and differences, we come together in our belief in the risen Lord, in our shared celebration of Eucharist. It is a sacramental reality that, all too often, has yet to be realized in our everyday life. It is the "already" and the "not yet" of the kingdom of God.

Every time we celebrate the Eucharist we are facing a mission, an ideal to be realized, a task to be fulfilled, a community to be built. The Eucharist asks that we take personal responsibility for realizing the body of Christ in our world today.

In a text quoted in the *Catechism of the Catholic Church* (#1397), John Chrysostom speaks about this task.

You have tasted the Blood of the Lord, yet you do not recognize your brother [sic]....You dishonor this table when you do not judge worthy of sharing your food someone judged worthy to take part in this meal.

This does not mean only that we should be merciful to the starving people of our world or comfort the suffering and those who grieve. We should do this and more without any doubt. But we must also be interested in and engaged in the establishment of the reign of God through our daily words and actions, through our political beliefs, and through our outreach to needy people around the globe.

Every time we say the Our Father, we pray, "Your kingdom come!" As we say this prayer, we should hear it as a call to mission, a mandate to live and work toward the fulfillment of this kingdom.

There is a dynamic tension implicit in the body of Christ that is sometimes misunderstood. Here is an example. In the 1960s, a Latin American priest named Camillo Torres decided that he could not celebrate the Eucharist in a situation where the difference between the rich and the poor was simply too great, as it was in his country. He thought that celebrating Mass in this kind of situation was hypocrisy.

His friend, the well-known theologian Gustavo Gutierrez, tried to convince him that his reasoning was theologically flawed. Gutierrez told Torres that to not celebrate the Eucharist would mean taking away the dynamic tension it creates. That tension, between the "already" and "not yet" of the kingdom of God, is what offers and guarantees our Christian hope.

But Camillo did not listen to his friend. He joined a guerrilla group and died in battle some weeks later.

FOR REFLECTION

- What does being a member of the risen body of Jesus Christ mean to you? How does it affect your daily decisions and activities?

- When you attend Mass, are you aware of the Eucharist being "already" and "not yet"? How and where do you see the kingdom in the world around you?

- What concrete steps might you take to assume personal responsibility for realizing the body of Christ in our world, for working toward the fulfillment of the kingdom of God?

MORNING PRAYER

Jesus, you came among us to restore unity to our human family.
Let me remember your commandment, and love God above all
and my neighbor as I love myself.

FAITH RESPONSE FOR TODAY

As you go about your day, take the opportunity to affirm God's goodness in the people you encounter along the way.

"Has no one condemned you?"

Read John 8:1–11

The gospel story here is sometimes referred to as "The Adulterous Woman." We have to remember, however, that titles such as these are not part of the original text but rather have been adopted by those who have read and used the Scriptures down through the ages.

Take the stories about the seed. You don't find any of these in John's gospel, only in the synoptic gospels, especially Matthew. In Matthew's gospel Jesus tells five "seed" stories, almost always referred to as the parables of the sower and the seed. The stories start out with someone going out to sow seed. But when you read all five stories carefully you discover that the word "earth" is used more often than "seed" or "sower." The stories are about the sower and the seed, oh yes; but more interestingly, they are about the earth. In other words, the stories are not so much about "them"—the sower and the seed—but about us—the earth!

One aspect illustrated by these stories is the power that is invested in us. If you have an envelope or bag with seeds, you have the potential for those seeds to grow into plants or bushes or trees. Even the most gigantic trees come from one seed, from one small nut!

Yet until you put those seeds in the earth, nothing is going to happen. If you put those seeds next to a flowerpot or on top of a seedbed they will remain as dead. It is only when the seed is put into the earth that its power, the force and the energy of that seed, can grow and come to fruition. Thus, the parables of the seed are about the power inherent in the earth.

The story about the adulterous woman illuminates this point in a different way. The Scripture passage here is not so much about the woman who sinned, but about the people who brought her to Jesus. They wanted to catch him; they wanted not so much to kill the woman as to kill Jesus. Yet in both cases—the treacherous leaders as well as the adulterous woman—Jesus was determined to bring out the goodness hidden in each of them.

Picture the scene. It is early in the morning. Jesus has come to the temple to teach, and people are gathered around him. Suddenly a group of shouting men appear, pushing and pulling something. It is only when they draw nearer that it becomes clear they are not pushing and pulling some*thing*, but some*one*: a woman.

The woman has been caught in adultery by her neighbors. She looks disheveled, and she is probably afraid, ashamed, embarrassed, and in shock. She knows that her life is at stake. By her actions, she has risked being stoned to death, the punishment for adultery according to the law.

The noisy crowd of scribes and Pharisees make the woman stand in front of Jesus. They state their case, then ask Jesus their trick question: "Teacher, this woman was caught in the very act of committing adultery. Now in the law Moses commanded us to stone such women. Now what do you say?" They try to make him face a dilemma; whatever answer Jesus gives, he will be in trouble.

If Jesus had said, "You are right, go ahead and stone her," the leaders would have spread his words throughout the countryside, contradicting his role as healer and life-giver. If Jesus had said, "No, let her go," the leaders would have said that he was against the Mosaic law.

And so Jesus does not answer at first, but bends down and begins to write on the ground with his finger. He does not look at the woman in order to save her from more embarrassment.

Jesus finally straightens up and says to the scribes and Pharisees: "Let anyone among you who is without sin be the first to throw a stone at her." He then bends down again and continues doodling in the sand. This answer puts the ball back into the court of the Jewish leaders. It shows compassion for the woman without condoning her sin; it also gives the leaders an answer that cannot be used against Jesus.

But Jesus does more than that. He appeals to the goodness of the scribes and Pharisees, notwithstanding their evil intentions, when he tells them, "Let anyone among you who is without sin"—in other words the one among you who is good—"be the first to throw a stone at her." Thus, the issue takes on a completely new perspective: how could anyone good, anyone sinless, throw a stone at another human being?

The eldest among the accusers understands first. One by one they drop the stones which they hold in their hands, and leave. Each one follows in turn, until there is no one left standing there but the woman and Jesus. He finally stands up and looks at her. She must understand by now that although this man does not condone what she has done, he nevertheless will be merciful to her.

Jesus says to the woman, "Has no one condemned you?" She replies, "No one, sir." And Jesus says, "Neither do I condemn you. Go your way, and from now on do not sin again."

Jesus treated the woman as he had treated the people who brought her to him. He affirmed her capacity for goodness. He trusted her, and he sent her home. He let her know that she was good in his eyes so that consequently she would be so in her own eyes.

This story is more than one woman's story. It is my story; it is your story. It tells of mercy and forgiveness, along with an appeal to the goodness inherent in each of us, breathed into us from the beginning of our existence. It is the story of our Savior not giving up on us.

FOR REFLECTION

- Reflect on the idea of Jesus as one who affirms, not as one who condemns. How might you become such a person to your family, coworkers, friends, and others in your community?

- Have you ever "condemned" someone through prejudice, gossip, or even lies? What might Jesus say to you about this?

- If possible, receive the sacrament of reconciliation this week. Seek the healing power of God's mercy and forgiveness.

EVENING PRAYER

Jesus, you were merciful to the woman caught in adultery.
Look mercifully on my failings and shortcomings.
Help me to forgive others as you forgive me.

"I am the good shepherd."

Read John 10:1–39

Jesus gives himself many names in John's gospel. He calls himself the bread of life (6:35, 48), the bread that came down from heaven (6:41), the light of the world (8:12), the resurrection and the life (11:25), the way (14:6), and the true vine (15:1), to mention a few. Not all of these names are easy to understand. They are somewhat cerebral and abstract in their description of his person and his personality. They ask for explanations, and refer to older biblical texts.

When Jesus calls himself a shepherd, however, he holds a beautiful image before us. We see an actual person, the person of a good shepherd. This is who he showed himself to be when confronting the angry and hypocritical mob in this morning's meditation. At the same time, this image describes how Jesus related to the woman caught in adultery.

This image was foreseen by David, when he wrote in Psalm 23:

The Lord is my shepherd, I shall not want.
You make me lie down in green pastures;
you lead me beside still waters;
you restore my soul.
You lead me in right paths for your name's sake.
Even though I walk through the darkest valley,
I fear no evil
for you are with me;
your rod and your staff—they comfort me.
You prepare a table before me
in the presence of my enemies;
you anoint my head with oil;

my cup overflows.
Surely goodness and mercy shall follow me
all the days of my life,
and I shall dwell in the house of the Lord
my whole life long.

A disadvantage of this image of Jesus is that it seems to reduce us to sheep. Sheep, known and named by the shepherd but nevertheless sheep, more or less meekly follow a shepherd. But this is not what Jesus intends when he uses that imagery. Go back to the story of the woman caught in adultery. Jesus appeals to her inborn inclination to lead an upright life, and asks her to sin no more. He suggests what should be done, but the decision to do so remains the woman's. He leaves the initiative to her.

When Jesus calls himself a good shepherd, he wants us to consider this in light of his relationship with us. He knows us by name, and we recognize his voice. In the other gospels we learn what the shepherd—the good shepherd—does when one of his sheep is lost. He leaves the rest of the flock to look for the lost one.

We might wonder if a shepherd would really take the risk of leaving ninety-nine sheep alone to look for the one that has been lost. It's possible that the lost sheep is just a maverick, one that will cause trouble again and again. Why not just forget about it and leave it to its own caprice? Isn't it a bit crazy to bother about one lost sheep? But that is exactly what is implied by this story, particularly as recounted in the gospels of Luke and Matthew; that is, Jesus has a crazy, unconditional love for all of us!

In John's gospel Jesus goes further than that. He is not only going out to find us, he is willing to lay down his life for us, the sheep:

This is why the Father loves me, because I lay down my life in order to take it up again. No one takes it from me, but I lay it down on my own. I have power to lay it down, and power to take it up again. This command I have received from my Father.

Further on in John's gospel, Jesus would say the same thing in another way: "No one has greater love than this, to lay down one's life for one's friends" (15:13).

Jesus speaks in an active sense about laying down his life. It is something he is going to do, not only something others are going to do to him. In other words, Jesus remains in control. He lays down his life in love for all. We find here the reason why Jesus was willing to pass through death for us. In John's gospel, Jesus dies not to pay a price to the Father but to join us in our human condition. Thus he introduces us to a new life, a share in God's life and love for all of us and for the whole of creation: "I came so that they might have life and have it more abundantly" (10:10).

Here we come to a second point in our meditation on the good shepherd. That name not only tells us metaphorically who Jesus is, it also tells us who we should be, how we should relate to each other and to the whole of creation. We too should be good shepherds!

When you have attended a baptism, perhaps you have been struck by the words used at the anointing with water: "I am anointing you as Jesus was anointed, priest, prophet, and king." These words call us into the new life we share as Christians. They also imply our identification with the good shepherd.

As good shepherds, we must be willing to organize our lives in such a way that others may live. This is quite a mission if you consider our world—one where many of us live in plenty, while others simply do not have the means to live. To take on the issues of this world is a task we cannot face on our own but only in the community we form as disciples who share in the life of Christ.

FOR REFLECTION

- Is there an incident or a situation in your life where someone has been a good shepherd to you? What has this meant to you?

- How do you see your mission to be a good shepherd—at home with your family, at work with colleagues, and so on?

- What are one or two things you can do each week to become a better "good shepherd"?

MORNING PRAYER

*Jesus, you guide me through the valleys and dark places
of my life. Let me strive to shepherd others with the care
and compassion you have shown me.*

FAITH RESPONSE FOR TODAY

Is there a young person you know who might benefit from your guidance? Seek out the chance to share a hopeful word or uplifting thought with him or her today.

"He is calling for you!"

Read John 11:1–44; 12:1–30

The story today is not so much about Lazarus as it is about his two sisters, Martha and Mary. Jesus was a family friend. As the story begins, Lazarus is very sick; he is dying. His sisters send a messenger to give Jesus the news in the hope that he will come to cure him.

Jesus receives the message and says, "This illness does not lead to death; rather it is for God's glory, so that the Son of God may be glorified through it." And so he does not go immediately to Bethany to see his friend. Instead, he stays two more days in the place where he is; only on the third day does he go. (So many things happen on the third day in John's gospel!)

Jesus tells his disciples, "Let us go to Judea again." His disciples do not want him to go: "Rabbi, the Jews were just now trying to stone you, and are you going there again?" Jesus answers, "Are there not twelve hours of daylight?" implying that as long as he is alive, he will work.

Jesus then tells his disciples that "Our friend Lazarus has fallen asleep but I am going there to awaken him." His disciples insist, "Lord, if he has fallen asleep, he will be all right." And so Jesus must tell them plainly, "Lazarus is dead. For your sake I am glad I was not there so that you may believe." Thomas speaks bravely, telling the others, "Let us also go, that we may die with him!"

When they arrive in Bethany, they find that Lazarus has been dead for four days. Martha and Mary are at home, surrounded by mourning family and friends. When Martha hears that Jesus is on his way, she goes to meet him, while Mary remains at home.

Martha says to Jesus, "Lord, if you had been here, my brother would not have died. But even now I know that God will give you whatever you ask of him." Jesus tells her, "Your brother will rise again." Martha answers

"I know that he will rise again in the resurrection on the last day."

Then Jesus says: "I am the resurrection and the life. Those who believe in me, even though they die, will live, and everyone who believes in me will never die. Do you believe this?"

Martha answers him, "Yes, I believe that you are the Messiah, the Son of God, the one coming into the world."

Then Martha goes back home, calls her sister aside, and tells her, "The Teacher is there, and is calling for you!" When she hears this invitation, Mary gets up quickly and goes to meet Jesus.

Why did Mary wait for that invitation? Why didn't she go out with her sister Martha when they first received word that Jesus was on his way?

When Martha meets Jesus she treats him as a family friend. She takes him to task for not having come sooner, but adds, "I know that God will give you whatever you ask of him."

Mary behaves in a different way. Meeting Jesus, who had called for her, she kneels at his feet, and she says what Martha had said to Jesus: "Lord, if you had been here my brother would not have died!" But she does not add that Jesus' prayer to God would be heard. Why? Perhaps Mary recognizes the divine presence in Jesus himself.

Mary weeps as she speaks to Jesus. Seeing her cry, Jesus too begins to weep. He asks, "Where have you laid him?" The people around begin to murmur, "Could not he who opened the eyes of the blind man have kept this man from dying?"

At the tomb Jesus tells them: "Take away the stone." Martha expresses a certain hesitation: "Lord, already there is a stench because he has been dead four days." Jesus tells her: "Did I not tell you that if you believed, you would see the glory of God?" So they take the stone away.

Jesus first turns his eyes upward and prays to his Father. Then he cries out in a loud voice: "Lazarus, come out." The dead man comes out, and Jesus says, "Unbind him and let him go."

When you read a story like this, you always—more or less spontaneously—identify with one of the persons in the story. You might recognize yourself in Lazarus, the dead person brought back to life by Jesus, the one buried in a cave with a stone in front of its entrance. You might put yourself in the place of Martha, the one who hesitates, the one who doubts. You might also put yourself in the place of Mary, the one whom Jesus called for. In another gospel story, Mary is the one who, according to Jesus, "has chosen the better part, which will not be taken away from her" (Lk 10:42). She truly loved him.

Mary shows her love in the second gospel account which we read this evening, when Lazarus' household invites Jesus for dinner. While Martha is serving, Mary takes a pound of costly perfume made of pure nard and anoints Jesus' feet, wiping them with her hair. "The house was filled with the fragrance of the perfume."

Jesus must have had a great love for this family. And each of them—Lazarus, Martha, and Mary—definitely loved Jesus, though all expressed their love in different ways. Isn't this a bit like us?

Some years ago, I was present at a family retreat, an intergenerational event for some seventeen families. The question was asked; "What would you do if you met Jesus?" Initially, no one was willing to respond. Then someone, an older person, said: "I would fall on my knees in front of him." Someone else thought she would try to get away as quickly as possible, afraid of the encounter, feeling unworthy. Another one remembered the prayer: "Lord, I am not worthy to receive you!"

Then a lovely redheaded girl, about twelve years old, put up her hand and shouted, "Me, me!" When everyone looked at her, she said: "I would go to him and hug him." She, too, would choose the better part.

It is love that counts; the rest is gravy.

FOR REFLECTION

- How would you respond to the invitation: "The Teacher is there, and is calling for you"? Have there been particular moments in your life when you have heard such an invitation?

- With which of the three main characters in these two gospel stories—Lazarus, Martha, or Mary—do you most identify? Why?

- Jesus' last question in John's gospel is "Do you love me?" What is your answer? How do you show this concretely in your daily life?

EVENING PRAYER

Jesus, let me choose the better part as Mary did in her relation-ship with you. Let my love for you be my lodestar in life.

"To gather into one
the dispersed children of God."
Read John 11:45–53; 12:20–36

The resurrection of Lazarus had a great impact on the people who followed Jesus. More and more people now came to hear him. The crowd often became so large that the high priests and the Pharisees were alarmed. Large crowds posed a danger to law and order, as well as to the authority of the leaders. The Romans would not like this situation either, as it might lead to a riot.

So the chief priests and Pharisees called a meeting of the council. Caiaphas, the high priest that year, presided. They were unanimous in their opinion: "This man is performing many signs. If we let him go on like this, everyone will believe in him, and the Romans will come, and destroy both our holy place and our nation."

Caiaphas was clear in his opinion of the other council members: "You know nothing at all! You do not understand that it is better for you to have one man die for the people than to have the whole nation destroyed."

The author of John's gospel goes on to tell us that, speaking prophetically, Caiaphas was right. The gospel recounts that "Jesus was about to die for the nation, and not for the nation only, but to gather into one the dispersed children of God."

Jesus was going to lay down his life not only for one group of people, not only for one nation, but for the whole of humanity and by implication, the whole of creation. His love, the love we share, extends to all and everyone. Jesus laid down his life so that we might share in that love—the divine love. It is the life he gave us.

Popular devotion, spirituality, and theology often reduce the reason for Jesus' death to our own personal and individual salvation. It is true that Jesus died for you, for me, for us. But we can overstate that truth to the point where it becomes a reduction of the full meaning of Jesus' life, death, and resurrection. John's gospel goes further in interpreting the meaning of this paschal mystery.

We find this broad interpretation of redemption in the story that follows the account of the meal at Lazarus' house in chapter twelve. Some Greeks who have come to the festival approach Philip and say to him, "Sir, we wish to see Jesus." Philip seems to hesitate. He does not say, "Yes, come with me," but goes to consult Andrew. We might imagine that the two discussed the issue before they finally decide to tell Jesus.

Jesus' reaction is interesting, even astonishing. He does not say, of course, "Wow, Greeks!" Yet, in a sense, that seems to be his reaction when he says, "The hour has come for the son of man to be glorified." It is as if things are falling into place.

Here we might understand what is happening in light of Caiaphas' prophecy. In those days, the Greeks were not political enemies of the Jews but their cultural opposites. It was the case of a pagan influence—the Greek culture—threatening the religious culture of the Hebrew nation. This may have been why Philip is reluctant to bring the Greeks to meet Jesus. Yet this hesitancy might also have been the reason Jesus tells them to open their circle:

> Those who love their life will lose it, and those who hate their life in this world will keep it for eternal life. Whoever serves me must follow me, and where I am, there will my servant be also....Now my soul is troubled. And what should I say—"Father, save me from this hour?" No, it is for this reason that I have come to this hour. Father, glorify your name.

At that moment heaven opens and the voice of the Father is heard affirming Jesus' words. Then Jesus adds, "Now is the judgment of this world; now the ruler of this world will be driven out. And I, when I am lifted up from the earth, will draw all people to myself." He says this to indicate his impending death.

"I will draw all people to myself." In these words Jesus expresses once more the universal character of his mission, to "gather into one the dispersed children of God" (11:52). This passage marks one of the most solemn moments in John's gospel, an unparalleled epiphany indicating what it means for Jesus' disciples to share in his life and love.

All through our history the followers of Jesus have had difficulty in living this love. All too often Christians have reacted negatively to those outside the circle of faith. Some Western nations that consider themselves Christian—those called to share in God's love by their hospitality to all—are the least welcoming to those they consider "others."

Yet Jesus laid down his life and took it up again because of his love, God's love, for all. Likewise, we must all actively and consciously participate in his mission of gathering together the dispersed children of God.

FOR REFLECTION

- Do you agree with those who say that there are no "others," that we are all one in God? How does this belief influence your life?

- Do you consider yourself to be a good and welcoming neighbor? What specific qualities or characteristics make you so?

- Reflect for a while on the peace and justice implications of being a disciple of Jesus and sharing his love for all. How might you do this in practical, daily ways?

MORNING PRAYER

Jesus, let me open my heart to the joys and sorrows of people I so often consider strangers to me. Help me to know and share the vision of your unending love for all the world.

FAITH RESPONSE FOR TODAY

If anyone today starts to tell you about their troubles or concerns, give them your time and listen to them. Encourage them by sharing an experience of your own life and faith.

"Do you know what I have done for you?"

Read John 12:1–8; and chapters 13; 14; 15; 16; 17; and 18:1

Jesus knew what was going to happen; it was no surprise when the soldiers came to arrest him. He knew that the leaders of his day did not accept the new life of God's love for all that he came to introduce.

Jesus was too much of a threat to the existing disorder in the world, and so he had to disappear. He was prepared to face their challenge.

Someone else knew intuitively what was going to happen to him: Mary of Bethany, his friend and the sister of Martha and Lazarus. In our meditation of the other day, we reflected on the dinner at the home of Martha, Lazarus, and Mary. As Martha served the meal and Lazarus sat at table with Jesus, Mary took a pound of very costly perfumed oil and anointed the feet of Jesus, drying them with her hair.

One of the disciples, Judas Iscariot, the Judas who would betray Jesus, protested and said that the money spent on the oil could have been used to help the poor. John writes that he said this not because Judas cared for the poor, but because he, who was in charge of the community's money, would have liked to pocket it for himself.

Jesus understood Mary's gesture, and he said to Judas, "Leave her alone. She bought it so that she might keep it for the day of my burial. You always have the poor with you, but you do not always have me." Jesus not only foresaw what was going to happen, he was preparing his disciples for his death.

Following the dinner with the household of Lazarus, Jesus returns to Jerusalem. The crowd comes out to meet him with palm branches, but their shouts of "Hosanna!" do not deceive him. He knows that his passover is near.

Jesus has made arrangements for his last supper with the disciples. There he shows his love for them by washing their feet, and asking them—and us—to follow his example. He even washes the feet of Judas Iscariot, who would soon betray him. During the meal that follows he dips a piece of bread in the dish on the table and gives it to Judas as a last sign of his love. Judas takes it, but then leaves immediately. John adds ominously: "and it was night."

Jesus then tells the others at table with him that he no longer considers them as his disciples but as his friends. Likewise they should no longer consider themselves as his servants. He is their friend.

In John's gospel, Jesus addresses the disciples in long passages several times during the meal. He explains that his way of life is the only way to go: he is the way and the truth and the life.

Life is the main theme throughout this gospel. A check through the English translation will show that he uses this word over forty times!

Jesus tells the disciples that we share together in the life he lives. To explain this, he uses the metaphor of a vine. "I am the vine, you are the branches. Those who abide in me and I in them bear much fruit, because apart from me you can do nothing."

It is interesting to note that Jesus does not say that he is the vine and we are leaves or flowers. Though we are each unique and individual, we are branches; we are clustered together. We cannot face the task Jesus left us on our own but only together in community. We are branches on the vine, communities of individuals.

Jesus then assures the disciples that he will be victorious notwithstanding what will happen to him. He is going to lay down his life, but he will take it up again. The life he lives is God's life. It is the life to which he invites us.

Jesus tells the disciples that later on—after his death and resurrection—they will begin to understand. "A little while, and you will no longer see me, and again a little while, and you will see me." Then he prays to the Father for his disciples, which means that he is praying for all of us. He promises that we will be gifted with God's spirit, and that we will be able to do even greater things than he was able to do in his earthly days: "Very truly, I tell you, the one who believes in me will also do the works that I do and, in fact, will do greater works than these, because I am going to the Father" (14:12).

Together with him we are taken up in a process. Things are happening. The kingdom of God is—and will be—growing among us!

John does not speak about the breaking of the bread and the sharing of the wine as do the other gospels—and later, as Paul did in his letter to the Corinthians. As such, John's gospel does not directly refer to the institution of the Eucharist. But the whole of John's description of the last supper makes it clear that throughout the evening, Jesus and his friends formed a bond that made them one in him.

During this all, the disciples must have remembered how Jesus had called himself the bread from heaven, and how he had spoken of eating his flesh and drinking his blood.

When the meal was over, "he went out with his disciples across the Kidron valley to a place where there was a garden, which he and his disciples entered." In the book of Genesis a garden is the scene of the beginning of humankind. Throughout human history, gardens have been considered therapeutic, healing places of meditation and conversion.

Jesus was going to be betrayed in a garden. Finally, he would be buried in a garden. But remember: he rose in a garden, as well!

FOR REFLECTION

- If possible, take some time today to sit in a garden or in a park. Breathe deeply and relax. Observe what is around you. Meditate on what happened in the garden on the night of the last supper.

- Have you ever been betrayed, let down, or deeply disappointed by someone? How did you handle this?

- What do you think Jesus meant when he said, "the one who believes in me will also do the works that I do and, in fact, will do greater works than these"?

EVENING PRAYER

Jesus, you have done great things for me.
Help me each day to continue your mission in this world.

"Why do you strike me?"

Read John 18:2–40; 19:1–42

The disciple who had left them during the last supper, Judas Iscariot, interrupts Jesus and the other disciples while they are at prayer in the garden. He guessed that they had gone there to pray, and he comes with a band of soldiers and temple police.

Jesus, who knew all that would happen to him, asks: "Whom are you looking for?" This question will be asked by Jesus twice again in John's gospel. When they reply, "Jesus of Nazareth," Jesus responds with one word, a Greek word meaning simply, "I am." He does not add anything to that verb. He does not qualify it by adding rabbi or prophet, just "I am he." It was the same answer God gave to Moses when he spoke to him from the burning bush (Ex 3:14).

When Jesus speaks this word, the whole cohort, including Judas, draws back and falls to the ground. Jesus again asks who they are looking for. Again they reply, "Jesus of Nazareth." Jesus tells the soldiers, "I told you that I am he. So if you are looking for me, let these men go."

Peter reacts strongly, draws his sword, swings it around, and cuts off the right ear of Malchus. Jesus says, "Put your sword back into its sheath. Am I not to drink the cup that the Father has given me?"

So the soldiers and the Jewish police arrest Jesus, bind him, and march him to the high priest's residence. They bring him first to Annas, the father-in-law of Caiaphas, the high priest, the one who had advised his council that it was better "to have one person die for the people."

Two disciples follow Jesus, one of whom is Peter. The other disciple, who is not named, seems to know the in-and-outs of the high priest's courtyard, and he gains access there for himself and Peter.

The story then starts to alternate between what happens to Jesus as he stands in front of the high priest himself, and what happens to Peter in the courtyard. So John's passion story is not only about Jesus but about the disciples, as well! It is also a story about you and me.

Notwithstanding his bravery with the sword, Peter's shadow side appears in this account. He betrays Jesus three times: when he enters the courtyard and the woman at the gate interrogates him; when he warms himself at the fire; and finally, when a relative of Malchus, whose ear Peter had cut off, recognizes him. Three strikes!

When Jesus is struck in the face by one of the police, he asks him: "Why do you strike me?" Jesus might well have asked Peter this same question, three times. In a way he did that much later, when three times he asked Peter, "Simon, son of John, do you love me?" (21:15–17).

Let's go back to the drama unfolding with Jesus. Caiaphas has sealed Jesus' fate, but since he is not authorized to put anyone to death, he sends Jesus to Pilate, the local Roman commander. During his interrogation by Pilate, Jesus does not hesitate to explain that he has come to introduce the reign of God into this world. When Pilate asks whether Jesus considers himself a king, Jesus tells him that his kingdom is not of this world. The kingdom to which he refers testifies to the truth about the world and its reality.

Afraid and at the same time pitying Jesus, Pilate tries to dodge responsibility for Jesus' assassination by offering to exchange him for Barabbas, a bandit. When that ruse backfires, he has Jesus flogged, hoping that this might appease the crowd. It does not.

Finally, though hesitant, Pilate gives in to the demands of the crowd, calling Jesus "king." And although the chief priests protest, Pilate has that title attached to the cross on which Jesus dies, in three languages: Greek, Latin, and Hebrew. Pilate makes certain that Jesus will die like a king. So does the author of John's gospel. He does not describe Jesus' death on the cross as a humiliation but as a coronation, the crowning of the task that Jesus came to accomplish.

Seeing his mother and the disciple whom he loved near the cross, Jesus entrusts his beloved disciple to his mother and his mother to his friend with these most beautiful words: "Woman, here is your son....Here is your mother." Then, in order to fulfill Scripture, Jesus says that he is thirsty. They take some sour wine and offer it to him on a branch of hyssop. After that, Jesus says, "It is finished." Scripture continues, "Then he bowed his head and gave up his spirit."

Some commentators who have studied these words do not agree with the translation "he gave up his spirit." They feel that this phrase does not do justice to the Greek word used in the original text. The words seem to imply that Jesus gave up his spirit to the Father. But the Greek verb indicates not a "giving up," but more a "giving through," a sense of passing on or handing over not to the Father but to those near the cross—his mother Mary, the beloved disciple, Mary Magdalene, and two other women, all of whom represent and prefigure the community that would form itself around him, a community enlivened by Jesus' spirit, life, and love.

In the moment when Jesus states, "It is finished," he reignites a fire that had been hidden in the ashes of human history. It was a moment not so much of con-version but of re-version. It symbolized a rebirth for the whole of humanity. Earlier in John's gospel, Jesus had used the metaphor of a woman in labor to describe his death (16:20–21). It would be like childbirth, creating for us the way to participate fully in God's life, to share in God's love.

Jesus' last words on the cross not only indicate an end, a completion. They are also a shout of triumph: it is accomplished! The old has been restored; sin has been overcome; death has been conquered.

FOR REFLECTION

- What is your feeling about being reborn yourself through the passion and death of Jesus? How do you identify with the passion and death of Jesus at this time in your life?

- Imagine that you are the beloved disciple, standing with Mary at the foot of the cross. What does it mean to you to hear Jesus say, "Here is your mother"?

- Through our baptism, we share in the life, death, and resurrection of Jesus. What difference has baptism made in your life?

MORNING PRAYER

Jesus, through my baptism I share in your living and dying.
Through you, I help give birth to a new humanity.
Give me the courage to share in this, no matter what the cost.

FAITH RESPONSE FOR TODAY

If possible, pray the Way of the Cross in church or at home. Reflect on the passion of Jesus and on the ways you walk this passion with him.

"Woman, whom are you looking for?"

Read John 20:1–18

The words Jesus speaks to Mary Magdalene at the tomb echo the first words spoken by Jesus in John's gospel: "Whom are you looking for?"

These words were spoken to a woman who is sometimes confused with Mary, the sister of Lazarus. Luke writes of "Mary, called Magdalene, from whom seven demons had gone out" (8:2). She was present at Jesus' crucifixion, and she was there when Joseph of Arimathea took Jesus' body from the cross. She had seen how Jesus was buried in a tomb in which no one had ever been laid, and how a stone had been rolled in front of his tomb.

Our story today starts out early in the morning, as soon as the Sabbath is over. It is still dark when Mary Magdalene enters the garden. She is obviously very sad, distraught, and looking for Jesus. She must have slept very little the night before. As a pious Hebrew woman, she may well have thought of the Song of Songs, sometimes called the holiest book in the whole of Hebrew Scripture,

Upon my bed at night
I sought him whom my soul loves;
I sought him, but found him not;
I called him, but he gave no answer. (3:1)

When Mary comes to the tomb she realizes that the stone in front of it has been rolled away. She does not investigate any further but runs to Peter and the beloved disciple to tell them what has happened. She must not have been alone in the garden, because she says, "They have taken the Lord out of the tomb, and *we* do not know where they have laid him."

Peter and the beloved disciple run to the tomb, with the beloved disciple outrunning Peter. He looks in the tomb and sees the burial wrappings, but he does not enter. Peter, however, does. He, too, sees the linen wrappings, even the carefully rolled-up cloth that had been covering Jesus' face. Could this have symbolized the secret that had veiled Jesus during his life and which is now taken away? A sign that he is now not only raised but also glorified?

The two disciples leave the tomb, and the text mentions that they believed. But what do they believe at this point in the story? Is it Mary Magdalene's report? Is it just the fact that the tomb was empty? Do they believe that Jesus has come back to life? That he has risen? John adds rather mysteriously that they do not understand as yet the Scripture that prophesied he must rise from the dead. This may have been the reason, John adds, that they just went home.

Mary Magdalene, who has returned with the disciples, stays at the tomb, weeping. Finally, she looks in. There she sees two figures dressed in white, two angels, who ask her why she is weeping. She answers, "They have taken away my Lord, and I do not know where they have laid him." She then turns around and sees Jesus, but she does not recognize him.

Jesus asks her the same question as the angels, "Woman, why are you weeping?" He adds a second question, "Whom are you looking for?"— that same question asked in the beginning of John's gospel, when Jesus asks Andrew and the other disciple, "What are you looking for?" (1:38).

Mary does not even recognize Jesus' voice. Her mind is on the emptiness of the tomb and Jesus' disappearance. In fact, she thinks that Jesus is the gardener, the one in charge of the tomb, and she says, "Sir, if you have carried him away, tell me where you have laid him, and I will take him away."

Jesus then says, "Mary." At this moment, when Jesus calls her by name, Mary recognizes him. She says to him "Rabbouni!" which means "teacher." Jesus calls Mary by her name. His relationship to her and her relationship to him are unique. That is why she recognizes him when called by her name.

It is the way Jesus relates to each one of us. He calls us not only by our given name, our official name, the name on our birth certificate or driver's license. He knows the name by which our mother calls us, and by which our friends know us. He knows the name that makes us feel at home, that really stirs our heart.

The good shepherd calls his sheep by name, our own name! I remember a nun who once told me that Jesus often spoke to her, never calling her by the name given her at her religious profession but always by the name with which her mother called her.

The intimate bond between Jesus and Mary Magdalene is confirmed in the rest of their conversation. He says to her, "Do not hold on to me, because I have not yet ascended to the Father. But go to my brothers and say to them, 'I am ascending to my Father and your Father, to my God and your God.'"

Note that Jesus no longer calls his followers disciples or friends; from now on they are his brothers and sisters! His Father is their Father, our Father; his God is their God, our God.

It is worthwhile for us to spend some time meditating on this early morning meeting in the garden. It is the morning of a new day, a new creation, one that has had a tremendous impact on human history.

Remember how we meditated this morning on Jesus who, as he died on the cross, handed his life, the divine life, on to those under the cross? He left them his breath! He left a life of love that we—members of his body—should be aware of, attentive to, and live to the full.

FOR REFLECTION

• Do you see everyone you encounter in your daily life as your brothers and sisters? Consider what it means to love these people with the love of Jesus.

• Think of times when you have heard Jesus's voice calling you by name. What does he say to you? What does he ask of you?

• In what ways do you announce to others that Jesus is our brother and friend? How does your life give witness to this?

EVENING PRAYER

Jesus, lift me up! You have conquered sin and death, and brought us to the joy of eternal life. I rejoice in your victory over death.

"He breathed on them."
Read John 20:19–31; 21:1–19

It was the evening of the day Mary had seen Jesus in the garden. His disciples are gathered together in a carefully secured house. Everything is locked. They are afraid of the people outside. But they may also be afraid of meeting Jesus, after the story Mary Magdalene had told them about seeing Jesus in the garden.

Suddenly, he stands in their midst. Not accustomed as yet to his risen body, they do not understand how Jesus has come in. While they hide their faces behind their hands, he says to them: "Peace be with you!" He then shows them his hands and his side. Their hands come down from their faces, and his peace fills their hearts.

The disciples are overjoyed. He has forgiven them; he has wished them peace! He has proven to be their friend, the healer of their broken hearts, the mender of their broken relationships, the restorer of their broken dreams.

To make sure he is not misunderstood, Jesus repeats his greeting, "Peace be with you! As the Father has sent me, so I send you." Then Jesus does what he has done to those standing under the cross at his passover. He breathes his life, his spirit into them and says, "Receive the Holy Spirit. If you forgive the sins of any, they are forgiven them; if you retain the sins of any, they are retained."

Jesus makes the disciples part of himself and gives them a share in his love. He tells them that they should forgive as he did, and what will happen if they do not forgive others. This is a natural outgrowth of the command found in John 13:34: "Just as I have loved you, you also should love one another."

Thomas is not in the room, and when they tell him the story he simply does not believe it. He wants some physical proof. He wants a test. He tells them that as long as he does not see the wounds in Jesus' hands and side, as long as he cannot touch the wounds with his own hands, he will not believe. You might call this "the Thomas test."

A week later, Jesus again appears to the disciples. This time Thomas is present, and Jesus gives him the Thomas test: "Put your finger here and see my hands. Reach out your hand and put it in my side. Do not doubt but believe." Thomas then makes one of the most radical faith statements in John's gospel when he exclaims, "My Lord and my God."

Although he was called "the doubter," Thomas left us a test we might well apply to all who call themselves disciples of Jesus. If you say you are one of his disciples, that you share in his spirit, his life, his mission, and his love, then let me see your hands and your side. If I see Jesus' wounds there because of the way you live in this world, I will believe.

After those initial appearances of Jesus, things slow down. The next story tells of Peter, who is gathered with six of his companions. Peter says to them, "I am going fishing." They reply, "We will go with you."

The disciples had been with Jesus for some time now. Yet it is as if they are returning to the life they had lived before they decided to follow Jesus. Could this be the same attitude of many of us, who, having had the insight and experience of Jesus' life and teachings through our baptism into Christian faith, continue to live as if nothing has happened?

Peter and the others spend the night on the lake but do not catch a thing. Rowing back to the shore at daybreak after this exercise in frustration, they see someone standing on the beach who asks them for some fish. They answer that they did not catch anything.

The mystery person then tells them to throw out their nets once more, to the right side of the boat. They do, and multitudes of fish swim into their net, so many that they have difficulty hauling the net back into the boat.

The beloved disciple suddenly understands, and he tells Peter, "It is the Lord." Peter, who had been naked, throws on some clothes and jumps into the sea. The others follow him to shore in the boat filled with fish, one hundred fifty-three large ones!

Jesus has started to prepare a meal for them, with a fire built and bread already baked. This will be their last breakfast with Jesus.

When they finish eating, Jesus asks Peter, the one who denied him three times in the courtyard of the high priest, "Simon son of John, do you love me?" Peter replies, "Yes, Lord; you know that I love you." Then Jesus says to him, "Feed my lambs."

This dialogue is repeated two more times. We can see that by the third time, Peter is beginning to be quite frustrated; he does not know where all this is leading.

Indeed, Jesus here confers a responsibility and power on Peter—and, by implication, on all of us who love Jesus and who are called to share in his divine love. He also qualifies that love for us.

Peter is told, and all of us through him, that our love for Jesus should show itself in genuine care for Jesus' people, for the whole of humanity and for the whole of creation. We, the carriers of his spirit and breath, are called to foster justice, peace, and integrity throughout the world.

Even the number of large fish caught in this story refers to this task. Some commentators think that the number one hundred fifty-three refers to the number of species of fish it was thought existed in that day. Thus, the fish would represent all of humanity with its different races, cultures, and ethnicities. This number tells us allegorically that we— together with Peter—share the task of the good shepherd, that is, gathering "into one the dispersed children of God" (11:52).

It's quite a task when you think about the racism, prejudice, and injustice rampant in the world today! But remember, our story tells us that "though there were so many, the net was not torn."

FOR REFLECTION

- Have you ever been aware of the Holy Spirit acting through you? When and where? What was the result?

- How does Jesus' spirit manifest itself now in your life—in your prayer, your witness, your work, and your relations with others?

- If Jesus were to say to you, "Feed my lambs," how might you respond? Name two concrete ways you can care for all of God's creation.

MORNING PRAYER

Jesus, you renewed God's Spirit in us by breathing your Spirit from the cross. Help me to receive it and live it.

FAITH RESPONSE FOR TODAY

With a friend, colleague, or spiritual advisor, share some of your thoughts about the spiritual journey you have been on for these past seven days. In what ways have you grown?

"Lord, where are you going?"

Read John 14:1–29; 21:20–25

Jesus is not the only one asking questions in John's gospel. So do his disciples—and so might we at the end of this retreat, trying to apply the graces we have received to our daily lives.

At the last supper, just before the end of Jesus' earthly life, the disciples had many questions. Peter asks straightforwardly, "Where are you going?" Thomas is more circumspect when he says, "Lord, we do not know where you are going. How can we know the way?" Philip tries a different approach and says, "Lord, show us the Father and we will be satisfied." Judas (not Iscariot) asks him, "Lord, how is it that you will reveal yourself to us, and not to the world?"

Jesus tells them that he is leaving them, returning to the Father. He tells them that his going away is, at the same time, a new coming. He explains that he intends to be with them, and consequently with us, in a new way. "I will not leave you orphaned, I am coming to you."

Yet the apostles are accustomed to being with Jesus in his physical presence, and it is this presence that will soon be gone. Think of what Jesus said to Mary Magdalene in the garden, "Do not hold on to me." He insists that they should be glad, not sad, because although he is leaving them he is going back to the Father. Further, he is going to send them the Spirit, who will be advocate, consoler, their future light. With that Spirit they will be able to do great things.

The Spirit will teach the disciples about sin and injustice, sanctity and righteousness. It will convince them about the final judgment, that Jesus has overcome evil and that although they would still have to struggle with sin, the final victory has been secured by him: "I have said this to you, so that you may have peace. In the world you may face persecution. But take courage; I have conquered the world"(16:33).

If Jesus does not go away, the Spirit cannot come to the disciples. "It is to your advantage that I go away, for if I do not go away, the Advocate will not come to you; but if I go, I will send him to you" (16:7). During the last supper, Jesus refers five times to that gift of the Spirit, to the presence of the risen and glorified life of Jesus in them.

This presence would in no way be inferior to Jesus' physical presence with the disciples as he walked, prayed, ate, and conversed with them during their days together in Palestine. His Spirit, his life, would abide with them; he would be in them, and they would know and experience the presence of Jesus in his Father, through the Spirit. The reality of his presence would not change, but the way in which he was present would. The disciples would have to pass over from knowing Jesus in the flesh to knowing him in the Spirit.

We, too, have to make this transition. When we receive communion, we receive Christ, the one who is risen. We do not receive Jesus as he lived before his passion, death, and resurrection. We receive the risen Lord, the one in whom all of us are incorporated. It is a reality that touches us both individually and personally.

An old legend tells about a monastery somewhere in the Christian past. In this place there were many personality clashes, jealousies, envies, and other all too worldly influences that left much to be desired in the life of the community.

One night the abbot had a dream. In it, an angel appeared to him and told him that the Messiah, Jesus himself, was a member of the community. The angel asked the abbot to keep this dream secret. But he did not keep the dream secret. Eventually everyone in the community became aware of the secret. No one, however, knew which of them was Jesus. Because they did not know, they began to treat each other very charitably. Their community life changed dramatically.

You can guess the moral of the story, right? Each one of the monks was Jesus. Each one needed to be reminded that "By this everyone will know that you are my disciples, if you have love for one another" (13:35).

Speaking of secrets, John's gospel hides one as well. Who is the disciple Jesus loved, the beloved disciple? We meet this person five times in John's gospel: he is sitting next to Jesus during the last supper (13:23); he is standing under the cross (19:26); he runs with Peter to the empty tomb (20:2); he recognizes Jesus on a foggy beach (21:7);

and he is there when Peter is asked to be a good shepherd and to follow Jesus (21:20). Perhaps he is also the one who, with Andrew, first followed Jesus (1:35). But the question remains, who is he?

This disciple mentions himself indirectly, when he ends the gospel by writing that the beloved disciple is the one who is testifying to all this; in other words, the one who is writing the book.

Why doesn't he mention himself by name? Was it only modesty? Or was there a deeper reason? Did the author want to be remembered as someone "loved by Jesus," the beloved of Jesus, in order for us to understand that we, too, are loved by him this way?

Whether or not this was the intention of the author of the gospel of John, it is a wonderful invitation for us to do just that. We should consider ourselves to be the beloved one. We can link ourselves to Jesus through the image of the beloved disciple, who remained with Jesus in good times and in bad.

Thus we can see ourselves as the beloved disciple, within the community of the beloved ones who remain with him until he comes again in glory.

FOR REFLECTION

- How do others know that you are a disciple of Jesus? Consider the practical steps you can take to make your daily life echo with Jesus' love.

- What does it mean to you that *you* are the beloved disciple? How might this affect your relationships with others?

- What is the most important insight you have gained during this retreat? How might this affect your day-to-day life?

EVENING PRAYER

The medieval mystic Meister Eckhart suggested that if the only prayer we say in our lifetime is "Thank you," it would suffice. And so we say… Jesus, thank you! Amen.

CONCLUSION

"May my joy be in you!"

Read John 15:11

It started with a sign, the wine provided by Jesus at Cana. In the Book of Ecclesiasticus, also called Sirach, we read, "What is life to one who is without wine? It has been created to make people happy. Wine drunk at the proper time and in moderation is rejoicing of heart and gladness of soul" (31:27–28).

A wedding feast is usually a time to rejoice. We celebrate the love between man and woman, husband and wife. And so it is fitting that "the first of his signs" (2:11) occurred at a wedding, a very joyful occasion, when Jesus changed six jars of water into wine. This joy continues to echo throughout John's gospel, mentioned again and again.

"I have said these things to you that my joy may be in you, and that your joy may be complete" (15:11).

"Your pain will turn into joy" (16:20).

"Your hearts will rejoice, and no one will take your joy from you" (16:22).

"Ask and you will receive, so that your joy may be complete" (16:24).

"[Father] I speak these things in the world so that they may have my joy made complete in themselves" (17:13).

Today, our sharing in the risen life of Jesus brings us joy. We experience the presence of Jesus in the abundance of life he brought us (10:10), the experience of the Spirit he sent us from his cross (19:30), and the peace with which he filled our hearts (14:27).

In the prologue to John's gospel we are told that the Word became flesh and lived among us. In this we see his glory, the glory of the Father's only Son, Jesus Christ, full of grace and truth. We too receive the fullness of his incarnation, grace upon grace.

We are an Easter people! We share Jesus' risen life! We belong together with him. He has called us brothers and sisters! We are God's own children; nothing in the world can come between God and us.

We have come to the end of our seven-day retreat. I hope this experience has left you spiritually refreshed, ready to be the living example of Christ in the world.

In the days that lie ahead, take a few moments from time to time to return to the gospel of John. Let it renew your being and remind you of the depth of Jesus' compassion and love for us. And may you be continually inspired and fortified in your efforts to bring the saving message of grace to all of our brothers and sisters throughout the world. Christ's mandate is a call for peace, justice, and the integrity of all the children of every nation.

May this retreat help you to realize this.

> *"I have said these things to you*
> *so that my joy may be in you,*
> *and that your joy may be complete."*

8/21/2010

Of Related Interest...

With Hearts on Fire
Reflections on the Weekday Readings of the Liturgical Year
Joseph G. Donders

A wonderful companion for homilists and those who participate in daily Mass.

0-89622-974-2, 352 pp, $19.95 (J-22)

God's Word Is Alive!
Entering the Sunday Readings
Alice Camille

Offers solid material for breaking open every reading of all three liturgical cycles, for Sundays an holy days alike. Includes reflection questions and points for action.

0-89622-926-2, 416 pp, $19.95 (C-02)

Between Sundays
Daily Gospel Reflections and Prayers
Rev. Paul Boudreau

Applies gospel truths to contemporary settings and challenges readers to be disciples of Christ here and now in everyday, accessible ways.

1-58595-169-2, 360 pp, $24.95 (X-05)

TWENTY-THIRD PUBLICATIONS
185 WILLOW STREET • PO BOX 180 • MYSTIC, CT 06355
TEL: 1-800-321-0411 • FAX: 1-800-572-0788
Bayard E-MAIL: ttpubs@aol.com • www.twentythirdpublications.com